BLUE WHALES

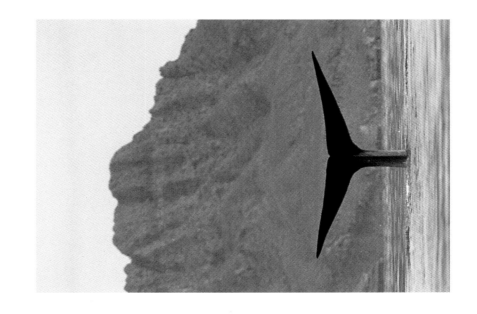

Printed in China

04   05   06   07   6   5   4   3

Library of Congress Cataloging-in-Publication

Calambokidis, John, 1954–
Blue whales / by John Calambokidis & Gretchen Steiger.
    p.   cm. — (World life library)
Includes bibliographical references.
ISBN 0-89658-338-4
    I. Blue whale.   I. Steiger, Gretchen, 1960–   II. Title.
III. Series.
QL737.C424C34   1997
599.5'248—dc21
                                                        96-39848
                                                        CIP

Published by Voyageur Press, Inc.
123 North Second Street, P.O. Box 338, Stillwater, MN 55082 U.S.A.
651-430-2210, fax 651-430-2211
books@voyageurpress.com   www.voyageurpress.com

Educators, fundraisers, premium and gift buyers, publicists, and marketing managers:
Looking for creative products and new sales ideas? Voyageur Press books are available at special discounts when purchased in quantities, and special editions can be created to your specifications. For details contact the marketing department at 800-888-9653.

Front cover © David E Myers (NHPA)
Back cover © Pieter Folkens
Page 1 © Marilyn Kazmers (Innerspace Visions)
Page 4 © Mike Johnson (Innerspace Visions)
Page 6 © Flip Nicklin (Minden Pictures)
Page 9 © François Gohier
Page 10 © François Gohier
Page 13 © François Gohier
Page 14 © Flip Nicklin (Minden Pictures)
Page 15 © Carolyn Gohier
Page 17 © Mark Conlin (Marine Mammal Images)
Page 18 © David E Myers (NHPA)
Page 21 © Paul Sterry (Nature Photographers Ltd)
Page 22 © Pieter Folkens
Page 25 © Flip Nicklin (Minden Pictures)
Page 26 © Flip Nicklin (Minden Pictures)
Page 29 © François Gohier

Photography Copyright © 1997 by:

Page 31 © Mike Johnson (Innerspace Visions)
Page 33 © Doc White (Planet Earth Pictures)
Page 34 © Pieter Folkens
Page 37 © Mark Carwardine (Still Pictures)
Page 38 © Pieter Folkens
Page 41 © François Gohier
Page 42 © François Gohier
Page 44 © François Gohier
Page 45 © Phillip Colla (Innerspace Visions)
Page 46 © Paul Sterry (Nature Photographers Ltd)
Page 49 © Tui De Roy (Oxford Scientific Films)
Page 50 © Flip Nicklin (Minden Pictures)
Page 51 © David E Myers (NHPA)
Page 53 © Tom Campbell
Page 54 © Flip Nicklin (Minden Pictures)
Page 57 © David O Brown (Passage Productions)
Page 59 © Mark Conlin (Planet Earth Pictures)
Page 60 © François Gohier
Page 61 © Tom Campbell
Page 62 © Pieter Folkens
Page 63 © Doc White (Planet Earth Pictures)
Page 65 © G. Steiger
Page 66 © Mike Johnson (Innerspace Visions)
Page 69 © Tui De Roy (Oxford Scientific Films)
Page 71 © François Gohier

BLUE WHALES

John Calambokidis & Gretchen Steiger

Voyageur Press

Contents

The authors gratefully acknowledge the many researchers and naturalists who have contributed to their research. Phil Clapham, Jay Barlow and Robert Brownell Jr. provided valuable comments on the text.

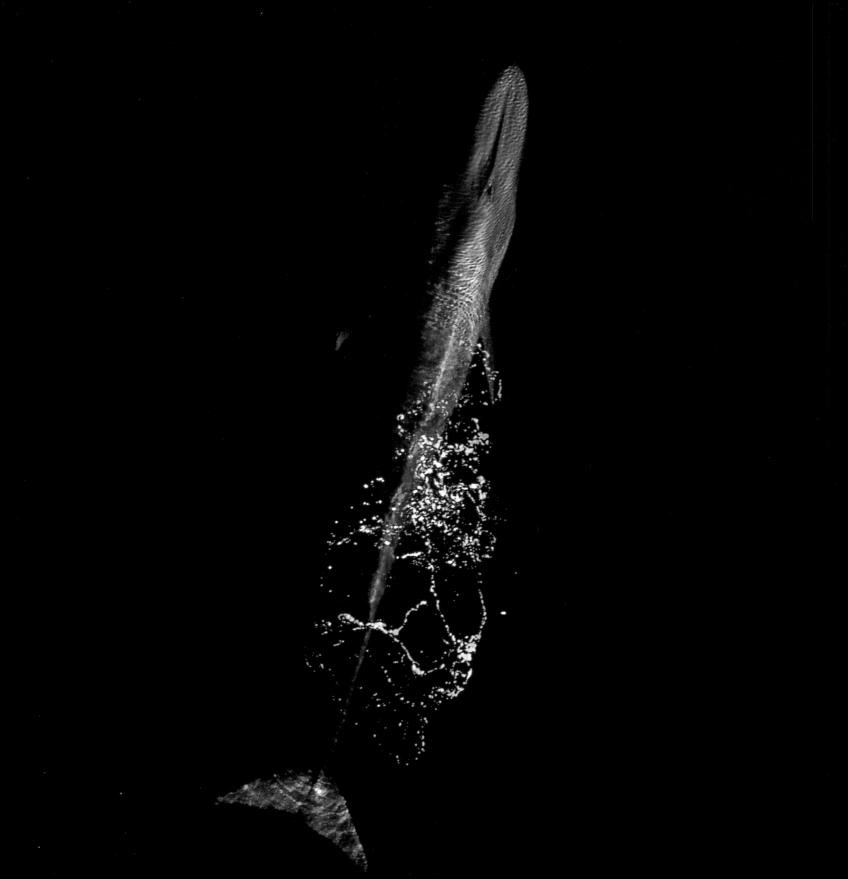

Blue Whales

There is no whaler and no whale biologist, no matter how experienced, who is so jaded that his heart does not race at the sight of a blue whale.

— Dale Rice, biologist at the National Marine Mammal Laboratory, Seattle

It is September and we are in a boat 30 miles (48 km) off the coast of California on a calm foggy day. The fog is dense, and I wonder how we will be able to find anything in this huge ocean. We turn the engine off and listen. At first the only sound is that of waves against the boat, then suddenly we are struck by the thunderous noise of a blue whale blowing at the surface. We head toward the noise and find the whale about a mile away. As we approach, its head breaks the surface, and we see the explosive white blow that reaches high into the air; its two blowholes are so big a toddler could crawl into them. Its light grayish-blue body is striking against the dark blue color of the sea. The broad U-shaped head disappears, and we can see only a portion of its enormous body. Its mottled back rolls through the water, and rolls, and rolls, and rolls, until finally its small dorsal fin comes into view. Behind the dorsal fin the thick tail-stock is visible, capable of powering the animal to bursts of speed as high as 20 knots. On its final surfacing, this blue whale raises its huge tail-fluke out of the water before disappearing into the sea.

The sight and sound of a blue whale surfacing in the sea is still breathtaking, even after spending the last ten years studying this species. Not that long ago, it was a sight that many feared would never be experienced again. Shortly after the hunting of blue whales had ended in the mid 1960s, it was thought that so few remained that extinction of this species was imminent. The first half of the twentieth century was marked by rapacious exploitation; modern whaling fleets efficiently stalked the seas and pursued and killed whales in all oceans of the world. Blue whale populations were decimated, first in the North

7

Atlantic, then the North Pacific, and finally in Antarctic waters. The killing was so intensive that George Small, in his book, *The Blue Whale*, which popularized the plight of this species, concluded:

The unrestricted slaughter that followed in the southern hemisphere resulted four decades later in the virtual extinction of the biggest animal that ever lived on the face of the Earth. The few blue whales remaining there, not yet free from the threat of man's explosive harpoons, cannot perpetuate themselves.

Fortunately, this dire prediction did not come to pass; although blue whale populations remain endangered and show little sign of recovery in most areas, there is also some cause for optimism. Blue whales in several regions are faring better than had been thought. Off the coasts of California and Mexico a surprisingly large population of blue whales has been discovered, which makes us hopeful that, although their populations are still at depressed levels, the species is no longer on the brink of extinction.

In our research, we have had the opportunity to study the California-Mexico population, which has astonished many scientists by its size. We first stumbled upon them while studying humpback whales off central California in 1986 and decided to take advantage of this opportunity to collect data on this rare species. Little did we know that they would become a primary focus of our work and we hardly imagined that we were studying the largest remaining population of blue whales left in the world! We feel privileged to have gained new information on the biology and population structure of this species which had largely gone unstudied since the end of whaling.

Here, we would like to share our excitement and insights into what is known about blue whales and recount some of the experiences we have had studying these amazing creatures.

8

Origins

Blue whales, like humans, are warm-blooded mammals which breathe air; give birth to live offspring, and nurse their young. They are classified in the Order Cetacea, which is divided into two groups: the odontocetes and mysticetes. The odontocetes, or the 'toothed whales,' comprise at least 65 species including dolphins and porpoises, killer whales and sperm whales. There are 11 species of mysticetes (which means 'moustached whale') also known as baleen whales; these animals use plates of baleen to filter their prey, and have no teeth. The mysticetes are further divided into three families: the Balaenidae, including the bowhead and right whales, which use a grazing method to feed (some classify the pygmy right whale in a separate family, the Neobalaenidae); the Eschrichtiidae, which is just one species, the gray whale, that often captures its prey with suction; and the Balaenopteridae, comprising the species that use a gulping method to catch their prey.

There are six of these 'gulping' species: the blue whale, fin whale, sei whale, humpback whale, Bryde's whale, and minke whale. They are characterized by the pleats in their throats which expand when they feed. This group is often referred to as rorqual whales; the word 'rorqual' comes from the Danish, meaning 'tubed whale'. They have streamlined, almost tube-shaped bodies, and are fast swimmers. All but the humpback whales have body characteristics similar enough to be classified in the same genus *Balaenoptera*. The scientific name currently accepted for the blue whale is *Balaenoptera musculus*.

There is some debate about the actual intent of the species name *musculus*. Carolus Linnaeus, the Swedish naturalist who was the founder of the modern classification system for plants and animals, gave blue whales this name in 1758. The Latin name *musculus* is the diminutive form of mouse (the scientific name for the house mouse is *Mus musculus*). Many believe that this was a humorous act by Linnaeus when he named the largest creature on

Earth. However, *musculus* also means 'muscular' (French from Latin), which is a more logical derivation for such a powerful animal. His intent is unknown; perhaps it was a clever pun.

Blue whales were first described by Robert Sibbald, a Scottish scientist, who examined a dead specimen that washed ashore in the Firth of Forth in 1692. This species was first given the scientific name *Sibbaldus sulphereus*. *Sulphereus* comes from the yellowish (sulfur) coloration on their bodies caused by a film of diatoms. These single-celled algae grow on the whales' bodies, and gives their white bellies a yellowish cast. Whalers often referred to blue whales as sulphur-bottomed whales.

Currently it is thought that there are three subspecies of blue whales: *intermedia* is the largest of all the blue whales and lives in Antarctic waters; *musculus* inhabits the oceans in the northern hemisphere and is somewhat smaller than its Antarctic counterpart; *brevicauda*, or the pygmy blue whale, is the smallest, and was first described in tropical waters of the southern hemisphere by Japanese scientists in the 1960s. Pygmy blue whales are no more than 80 ft (24.4 m) long, with shorter tails and longer bodies. In the next few years, genetic research and other techniques will help to clarify the differences between these groups.

Blue whales are closely related to fin whales, which are somewhat smaller and have a much darker coloration. Genetic tests were conducted on an unusual-looking pregnant female that was killed by whalers off Iceland in 1986. The animal had physical characteristics of both fin and blue whales, although its overall coloration and dorsal fin size were more like a fin whale. The tests revealed it to be a hybrid, the offspring of a blue whale male and a fin whale female. Genetic analysis of the fetus also showed that the hybrid mother had mated with a blue whale. Pregnant hybrids of any species are extremely rare, and the viability of this offspring is unknown.

The documentation of interbreeding between these two species may

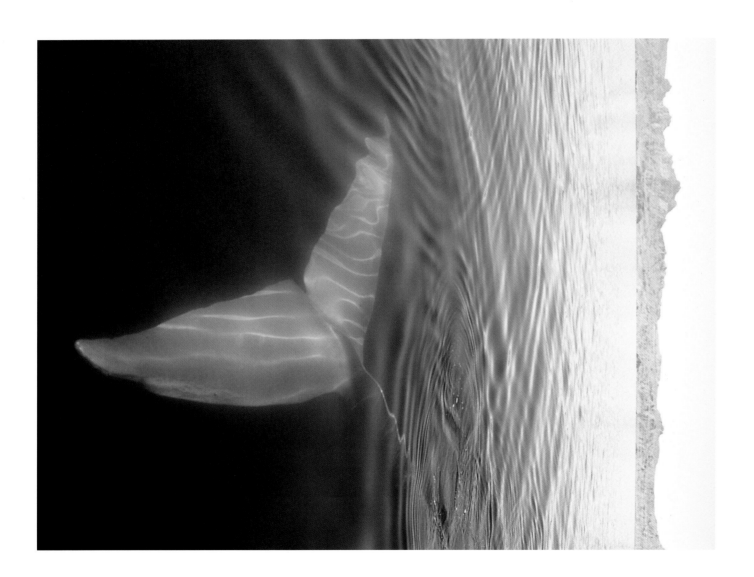

explain several very unusual sightings we have had over the years. The most dramatic occurred while we were studying blue whales far off the California coast. As we approached a cow and calf pair, we were surprised to see that the smaller animal looked more like a fin whale. Its body was dark brown and its dorsal fin was tall and falcate (sickle shaped). This animal was the size of a calf and stayed very close to the much larger blue whale. From both its size and behavior, we were certain that it was a calf but it certainly did not look like a blue whale. This calf may have been a hybrid of the blue whale mother which had mated with a fin whale, the species it most closely resembled.

We have also repeatedly seen an unusual animal which resembles a fin whale, with one exception: it does not have the patch of white on its right lower jaw that is a characteristic feature of this species. We have seen it often over many years; on every occasion, it has been in a group of blue whales, usually closely associated with one of them; they sometimes surface and feed together. In the absence of genetic evidence, we do not know the status of either of these whales but they may represent hybrid animals.

How did such a behemoth as the blue whale come into existence? The study of the origin and evolution of whales has been a difficult one, partly because of the large gaps in the fossil record. Recent findings have helped to complete this record, especially for the earliest periods of cetacean evolution.

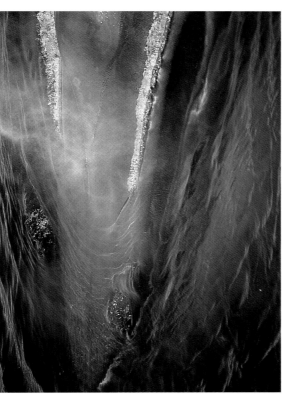

The U-shaped head breaks the surface.

New genetic techniques have also provided fresh evidence of the relatedness of whales to some groups of terrestrial mammals.

The evolution of the first whales began more than 50 million years ago. The extinction of marine reptiles left open a niche for a large marine predator. The earliest whales apparently originated in the warm shallow waters of the ancient Tethys Sea, roughly in the area where the Mediterranean Sea and Persian Gulf are now. In this fish-rich environment, a group of ungulates (hooved mammals) began exploiting the plentiful prey available. These terrestrial whale ancestors appear to be closely related to modern artiodactyls, a group that includes deer, camels and hippopotamus.

One of the earliest examples of a whale ancestor was the recently described *Ambulocetus*. This species, which provided one of the crucial 'missing links' in cetacean evolution, was apparently amphibious. It had features of ungulates including front and hind limbs that ended in hooves and a long tail. Features of the skull showed early characteristics of cetaceans and the animal apparently swam with an up-down undulation of its tail and rear legs, a motion similar to that of the tail-flukes of modern cetaceans.

The first fossil records of recognizable ancestors of today's baleen whales date from some 30 million years ago. These were members of families not in existence today. Just a little over ten million years ago the first Balaenopteridae, the family that includes blue whales, were seen.

In cetacean evolution, adaptations to the marine environment became progressively more specialised. The nares (nose opening) shifted to the top of the head which allowed whales to surface to breathe more efficiently. The rostrum (snout) telescoped forward creating a more streamlined shape and made it easier to catch prey. Appendages evolved into paddled-shaped fins. There were many other changes in their physiology and metabolism; they developed lighter bones, keener senses to detect prey, better oxygen-storing capabilities in their muscles and better ways to keep warm.

Whales evolved from terrestrial mammals and developed specialized features that allowed them to feed on dense concentrations of prey in marine waters.

17

Magnificent Giants

During the millions of years that life has existed on the earth many exotic animals have appeared. People generally think that the largest of them must have been some dinosaur of the Mesozoic Age. One of them, Brachiosaurus, was a giant that weighed an estimated 50 tons. But such a giant was a runt compared to a blue whale, which weighs 50 tons long before the age of puberty. Indeed, a large female blue whale can lose 50 tons while nursing a calf and still weigh twice as much as Brachiosaurus.

— George L. Small, *The Blue Whale*

More recent size estimates of *Brachiosaurus* put it at perhaps 80 tons, still about half the weight of a blue whale

Unquestionably, one of the most amazing aspects of blue whales is their immense size. An adult female can grow to a size that is longer than three typical buses put together end to end. She is heavier than an average group of 1500 people. Her tongue alone weighs as much as an elephant. The blow, almost three stories high (about 30 ft or 9 m), is expelled from lungs that weigh over a ton. Her tail-fluke is nearly as wide as a soccer goal. Her calf swallows at least 40 gallons (190 litres) of rich milk per day as it gains 9 lb (4 kg) an hour while nursing.

How long is the largest blue whale? It is difficult to sort out the accurate measurements from the big fish tales. Most size information was collected during whaling when large numbers of whales could be examined. Usually this information was collected by the whalers themselves, and standard zoological methods were often overlooked. Many factors affect the measurements, such as the position of the whale, and the shape of the flukes, which are flexible and were often cut off for towing. Biologists define the standard length of a whale to be a straight line measurement from the tip of the upper jaw, or rostrum, to the notch of the tail-fluke. Deviations from this method, as well as incentives to report large size, probably resulted in exaggerated lengths; one has to consider who made the measurement and how it was taken.

Most measurements of the largest blue whales come from the Antarctic in the first half of the twentieth century, when most whales were killed. There are records of two female blue whales killed before 1930 that measured 109 ft (33.3 m) and 110 ft (33.6 m); there is some dispute about the reliability of these measurements. Dale Rice, a biologist at the National Marine Mammal Laboratory, however, using only measurements made by scientists, concluded that the longest whale that could be verified was a 98 ft (29.9 m) long female taken by Japanese whalers in the 1946-47 season. Unfortunately, because most whales were not measured by scientists, this requirement may have excluded the largest animals. Given these uncertainties, a maximum length of about 100 ft (30.5 m) is the best to use. The blue whale is so large that its measurement does not require any unwarranted embellishment.

One thing that is clear is that the largest blue whale to ever live, and thus, the largest creature on earth, was a female. As for all the baleen whales, females are slightly larger than males; blue whale females are about 5 ft (1.5 m) longer. The largest female probably lived prior to or during the advent of modern whaling and her life may have ended on the flensing deck of a whaling station. Because the largest and oldest blue whales were the target of whalers, this class was virtually exterminated. Large size is an advantage for a female to meet the demands of growing and feeding a healthy calf that must survive in the cold ocean waters. In some toothed whales, such as sperm whales, males are larger than females, the result of a polygamous breeding system.

Blue whales in the Northern Hemisphere are somewhat smaller than their counterparts in the Antarctic. The longest blue whale taken in the North Pacific from shore stations in the United States and Canada was an 88 ft

20

It is often hard to comprehend their enormity until they swim under the boat.

A whale's blow hole is so large that a toddler could crawl into it.

(26 m) female. The length at which blue whales in the Northern Hemisphere reach sexual and physical maturity is also correspondingly smaller than in the Southern Hemisphere.

The process of weighing a whale, particularly a blue whale, has been described as a Herculean task. Of the hundreds of thousands of blue whales that were killed, relatively few were ever weighed. Whales were weighed piece by piece, resulting in the omission of the weight of blood and other fluids that were lost during the dismemberment process. Maximum weights have been reported to be about 160-190 tons; there was also some confusion because 'tons' referred to three slightly different units. All but two weights were of whales less than 90 ft (27m) long and the longest whales were never weighed. It is therefore reasonable to conclude that the largest blue whale probably weighed over 200 tons.

The blue whale is not only the largest animal that has ever lived, but is also one of the loudest. Blue and fin whales emit low-frequency moans, so low that they are below the range of our hearing, but they have been measured at about 185-190 decibels using scientific monitoring equipment. Because of ocean properties and the tendency of sound to be reflected off sharp gradients in the water, these sounds are sometimes audible for thousands of miles. Blue whales can hear each other and potentially communicate across entire ocean basins. Communication across such distances is unknown in any species except for the blue whale and its relative, the fin whale.

These sounds were heard for many years before it was even known they were the vocalizations of whales. Starting in the 1950s, military stations which had equipment capable of detecting and recording low-frequency sounds reported hearing very loud, low-frequency moans. The source of these was a mystery and it was not until the 1960s that some of them were positively identified as those made by baleen whales.

Blue whales can make somewhat different sounds depending on the

23

region and even the individual. Their vocalizations have generally been described as being primarily in the 15-20 Hz range and are therefore infrasonic because they are at or just below the lower limit of human hearing. These frequencies are similar to some of the vocalizations of elephants. Blue whale sounds generally consist of two components, sometimes with a break in between, each lasting about 10 seconds and repeating about every minute. The frequency of the second component is often lower or ends in a downward sweep.

How blue whales use these powerful underwater sounds is not known. Marine mammals use sound for a variety of reasons. Toothed whales use high-frequency sound as sonar to locate fine details about the location, size, and composition of prey and other objects nearby. Low frequency sound is not suited for this type of fine detail but may be useful for locating much larger features at great distances. On their breeding grounds male humpback whales sing complex songs that appear to play a role in attracting mates or warding off other males. Blue whale vocalizations may have a role in courtship, although at this point, it is not even known if one or both sexes vocalize.

Blue whales do not just make a lot of noise underwater. We have used the loud sound blue whales make above the water when they blow (breathe) to locate them either when there are calm conditions or when it is foggy. We can hear blue whales blow at the surface from several miles away, often before we can see them. Several times we have been startled by the intensity of sound generated by a blue whale blow when it surfaced unexpectedly just a few feet from our boat. The intensity of this sound results from the large volume of air being forced out of the blowholes under high pressure. Whales exchange 80-90% of the air supply in their lungs with each breath; in contrast, humans exchange only about 10-15% of their air.

While underwater, blue whales emit loud calls that carry thousands of miles.

Research Methods

Along the sides of a blue whale there is a mottled pattern of light and dark pigment in the skin. The pattern of this pigmentation is unique to each individual whale and does not change over time. By photographing this pattern on both the right and left sides of the whale, we can use these markings to identify and track it throughout its lifetime. Since the body of a blue whale is so large, we use the dorsal fin as a reference point and photograph the pigmentation in this region. This part of the body usually comes high up out of the water just before the whale dives. The dorsal fin is very far back on the whale, giving us plenty of time to focus our cameras as the long body rolls through the water. We also take photographs of the underside of the whales' tail-flukes when they raise them to dive, because sometimes these contain distinctive scars and markings.

Blue whales were first photo-identified by Richard Sears, a Canadian researcher with the Mingan Island Cetacean Study in Quebec. He began photographing blue whale pigmentation patterns in the Gulf of St. Lawrence in the western North Atlantic Ocean in the early 1980s. Our blue whale research off California began in 1986. Since then, we have identified 972 different individuals along the coast of California and Baja California. This collection includes photographs taken by biologists at our institution, Cascadia Research, along with those contributed by many other biologists and naturalists.

One example of the stability of this pigmentation over time was dramatically illustrated by photographs of a whale that has been seen over a 19-year time span. A biologist named Gary Friedrichsen sent us a photograph of a blue whale he had taken in December 1975 off Monterey Bay, California. We compared it to our collection and realized that it was a whale that we have seen regularly. There has been no visible change in the pigmentation pattern from 1975 to 1994, when our most recent photographs of this whale were taken.

27

This technique of photographic identification of individual animals has been conducted on a number of species of large whales. It has been used by researchers since the early 1970s with humpback whales, right whales and killer whales. With the ability to identify and track individuals over a long period of time, much can be learned about whale biology. By identifying whales in different regions, we learn about their migration and movements and the range of a population. When a whale is accompanied closely by a calf, we know that it is an adult female and can trace her reproductive history in successive years. The calves can be tracked in the future as known-age animals, whose behavior and social affiliations can be studied. Photo-identification methods can be used to estimate the size of the population using a technique called mark-recapture; the number of matches found between multiple samples of photo-identified whales provides an estimate of the size of the entire group (including the whales not identified).

Our photo-identification research begins with an intensive field season for several months each year. The large feeding range of blue whales requires us to be fairly nomadic. Because we cannot predict the movements of feeding whales, our schedule is flexible as we move to areas where large groups of whales congregate. We learned early in our work that small (18 ft/5.5 m) rigid-hulled inflatable boats were most effective for photo-identification because they are fast, seaworthy, and highly maneuverable around whales. We keep our boats on trailers so that we can rapidly move them to new regions when we receive sighting reports of whales. It is not uncommon for us to spend the day out at sea and the evening in a truck towing a boat to a new area which we think will be more productive.

Before dawn, we recheck the weather forecasts and current wind and sea conditions. When it is light, we launch our boat and begin the journey offshore towards the edge of the continental shelf. This area, rich with prey, is the best place to look for whales. Our commute is a long one because these regions

28

The different shades of pigmentation along a
blue whale's back, although subtle, form a distinctive pattern that allows
each whale to be identified. These patterns appear unchanged even in whales tracked
for twenty or more years. The shape of the dorsal fin and scars provide
additional unique features for identification.

are usually 20 miles (32 km) or more offshore. We slowly scan for whales and hope for a calm day. The height of the waves and the wind speed usually increase farther offshore. It is hard to search for whales when the swells rise to more than 8 ft (2 m) and obscure the view. When the wind is strong enough to cause the waves to break, it is even harder to spot a whale. Most mariners consider our boats too small to take so far offshore in these conditions, however they are well equipped for trouble with two navigational systems (GPS and LORAN), marine radios, a waterproof Emergency Locator Transmitter, and survival suits that would allow us to survive for days in these waters.

As the land disappears behind us, we are left with a feeling of the vastness of the ocean and the impossibility of our mission to find whales. Although we often know where whales have been in recent days and weeks, this is not a sure indication of where they will be today. Our primary study area off California extends more than 750 miles (1200 km) along the coast and 50 miles (80 km) offshore. It can feel like looking for a needle (albeit a very large one) in a haystack. We can search up to 200 miles (320 km) in a day. Then we see our first Cassin's auklets, small birds that also feed on krill. We can almost smell the krill in the air and then the sea becomes full of life.

A tall plume of mist on the horizon slowly disappears then reappears; it is the blow of a whale. From the height and spacing of the blows, we can tell that there are two blue whales. We record information on the time, location, whale behavior and bottom topography. The depth sounder shows that we are in 60 fathoms (110 m) of water and the bottom begins to drop off steeply; several dense patches of prey appear on the screen. When the whales surface, we slowly approach them from behind and to one side, positioning ourselves so that the sun is behind us and keeping our speed slow and steady to avoid disturbing them, yet close enough to get a full-frame shot of the side of a whale with a telephoto lens. We wait until the animals arch their backs during

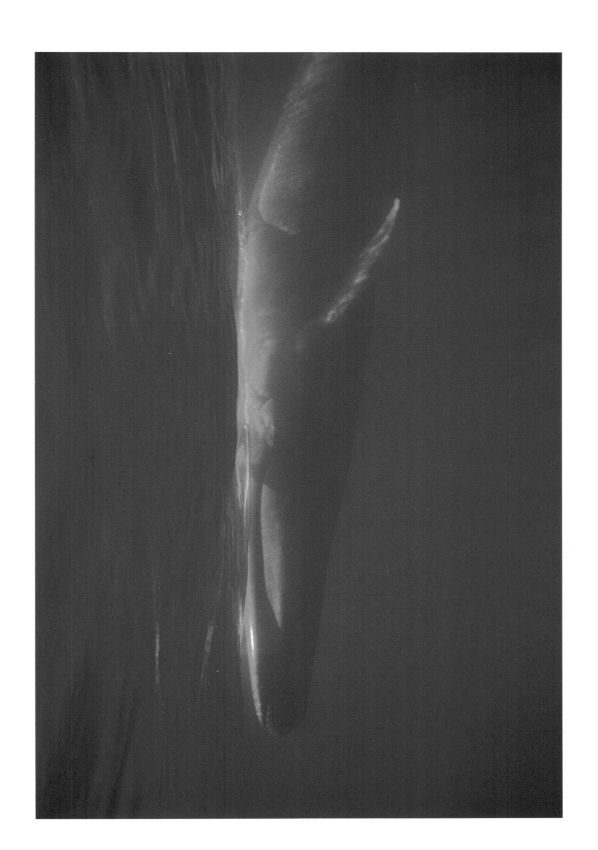

It is difficult to study the behavior of whales when they are underwater.

31

their final surfacing before diving to feed. As the small dorsal fin becomes visible we take a series of photographs showing the distinctive markings on this side. We use a black-and-white film at a high shutter speed; this is essential because of the continual motion of both the whale and the boat. The next time the whales come up we will repeat the process, this time to photograph the other side.

As we stay with this one pair of whales we continue to scan for others. Usually the whales are concentrated in one area where there is a high density of prey. After determining how they are distributed, we plan a route that will allow us to identify systematically as many of them as possible with minimal duplication. As we follow one whale, we notice that the water is suddenly brick red in the whale's wake. Whale feces! We put down our cameras and race to scoop it up with a dip net before it sinks. These samples will later allow us to determine what the animal has been feeding on.

Once we have sampled most of the whales in this aggregation, we move on and continue our search. We want to get a complete picture of how many whales are around. By the end of a long day being bounced around by the waves, our bodies are tired and our eyes are sore. The decreasing light brings some of the prey closer to the surface, and more whales are lunge-feeding, mouths open, at the surface. We watch the sun set with whales feeding all around us; then head back to the harbor in the dark. On shore we load our boat on its trailer and then it is time to check forecasts and sighting reports and decide where to drive to for our next day on the water.

Many of the harbors from which we launch – Trinidad, Moss Landing, San Francisco, – are locations of past whaling stations. Strangely, our mission has many similarities with those of past whalers. We have both faced the dangers of the sea in search of whales. The hunt by whalers was not with cameras but with harpoons, and driven by a search for profit that would threaten the very survival of the species.

Despite their bluish-gray pigmentation, whalers referred to this species as 'sulphur-bottomed' whales because many have a yellowish film of diatoms along their undersides.

33

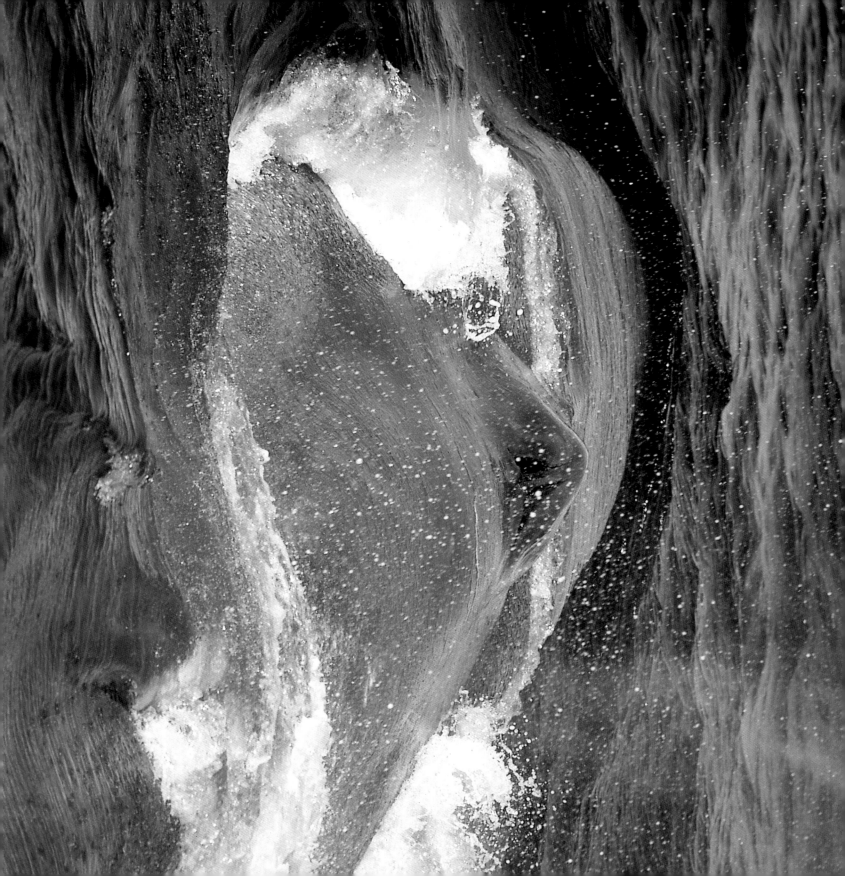

The Past

Early whalers knew little about blue whales, only that they were much too fast and powerful to be pursued, caught and killed. Their operations targeted species such as right whales and sperm whales, which were easier to catch with sail-powered whaling ships. Their boats needed to be able to approach whales to kill them with harpoons and lances thrown by hand. Another obstacle for whalers was that blue whales sank when they were killed, so the whalers would lose their catch, whereas right whales floated when dead, thus they earned their name as the 'right' whale to catch. The enormous size of blue whales also caused problems. One animal that whalers managed to tow to shore in Monterey Bay, California, was so large that it tore up all of their onshore rolling equipment. These whalers could salvage only the blubber that could be cut away from above the water.

Blue whales and their relatives remained out of the reach of whalers until the development of boats that could catch them, a weapon that could kill them, and a method that could keep them from sinking once killed. As numbers of the other target species began to decline and became hard to find, there was strong incentive to develop techniques to catch the faster rorquals. Although there were numerous developments on all these fronts, a Norwegian whaling captain, Svend Foyn, is largely credited with the crucial inventions that formed the foundation of modern commercial whaling.

In 1864, using funds from his success in sealing operations, Foyn launched the first steam-powered boat built specifically to catch whales. The boat did not meet with immediate success, however, because of reliability problems with the harpoons. He improved on existing designs and developed a harpoon with an explosive head that was fired from a swivel-mount cannon at the front of the boat. A strong rope attached to the harpoon secured the whale to the boat. When these techniques became sufficiently refined to be successful, whalers could, for the first time, target the swift rorquals. Blue whales were a primary target, but these operations also included fin, sei, and humpback whales.

Although unrestricted whaling of this type quickly diminished blue whale populations in the North Atlantic, the rapid development of modern whaling set the stage for the global expansion of this industry. Large whaling operations were established in the North Pacific, particularly in the Gulf of Alaska and off Baja California and Japan. Exploitation in the Southern Hemisphere was by far the most extensive, where, from 1904, whales were hunted from shore-based whaling stations.

By 1925, floating factory ships had become the most successful way to catch large numbers of whales. These ships, and their associated fleets of catcher boats, could go to areas where whales were concentrated, and could hunt and process the whales simultaneously. Although Norwegian companies dominated in the early 1900s, the United States, Great Britain and Japan were also prominent whaling nations.

Blue whales were the primary target of these floating factory ships. Although they accounted for just 15% of whales seen by whalers on the Antarctic feeding grounds before World War II, they made up a majority of the catch. Catches of blue whales peaked in the 1930-31 season, when 41 factory ships killed 28,325 blue whales; 8601 fin whales and 510 humpback whales were also taken.

The blue whale's streamlined body shape allows it to swim quickly and efficiently.

Since the (advent of modern whaling), it has been chased as no whale was ever chased before, and for decades hunters of the seas have prized the blue whale as the mightiest game on our planet.

— J.T. Ruud, Scientific American

In total, over 350,000 blue whales were killed worldwide, and 90% of these were taken in Antarctic waters. By the late 1930s, their populations began to decline. Hunting for blue whales became less profitable as they were harder to find and the catch consisted more and more of smaller, immature animals, so whalers shifted their focus to other whales. Fin whales, which had also been taken in substantial numbers along with blue whales, dominated the catch for about 20 years after World War II. As fin whale populations became depleted whalers shifted to progressively smaller rorquals, sei whales and then minke whales.

Unfortunately, whaling restrictions did not protect blue whales after their populations had collapsed. Catch quotas, determined in 1946 by an international convention for the regulation of whaling, were still based on an absurd measurement known as the 'blue whale unit' (BWU). This measurement was based on the amount of oil that could be extracted from a whale. Because about 20 tons of oil could be collected from one dead blue whale, compared to 10 tons from a fin and 8 tons from a humpback, one BWU equalled one blue whale or two fin whales or two-and-a-half humpback whales. Quotas set in blue whale units, without regard to the status of particular species, allowed whalers to deplete populations that were already in trouble. The lack of restrictions resulted in blue whales still being killed whenever they were encountered.

Blue Whales would only briefly escape whalers by diving.

Despite the fairly rapid depletion of blue whale populations in all areas where they were hunted, it was not until the mid-1960s that the hunting of this species was finally prohibited by the International Whaling Commission (IWC). The failure of this body to protect blue whales until they were commercially extinct was symptomatic of its inability to effectively manage whaling throughout its early years. Initially formulated at a conference immediately following World War II, the IWC consisted of representatives of all of the whaling nations.

This level of co-operation was unprecedented; virtually all of these countries were willing to turn over control of whaling, even in their own territorial waters, to a permanent international body. However, to preserve the power of individual nations, the provisions of the IWC charter allowed a country to exempt itself from any decision made by the IWC by lodging a protest; this meant each member country had the power to veto any decision. Additionally, recent revelations have shown that restrictions and quotas set by the IWC were sometimes ignored. For example, the former Soviet Union killed about 100,000 more whales than they had reported for the period 1948 to 1972, including over 8000 pygmy blue whales, as well as protected right whales.

The powerful short-term economic interests of whaling nations, combined with the impotence of the IWC, was the reason why protection and management of whale populations was such a dismal failure until recent years. It was only when non-whaling nations (including those that had ceased whaling) dominated the membership of the IWC that the organization finally fulfilled its responsibility of managing whale populations. In the last 10 years, the IWC has made decisions, some strongly contested by whaling members, which have promoted whale conservation. Economic threats from non-whaling member nations have been largely responsible for the adherence to decisions made by the IWC.

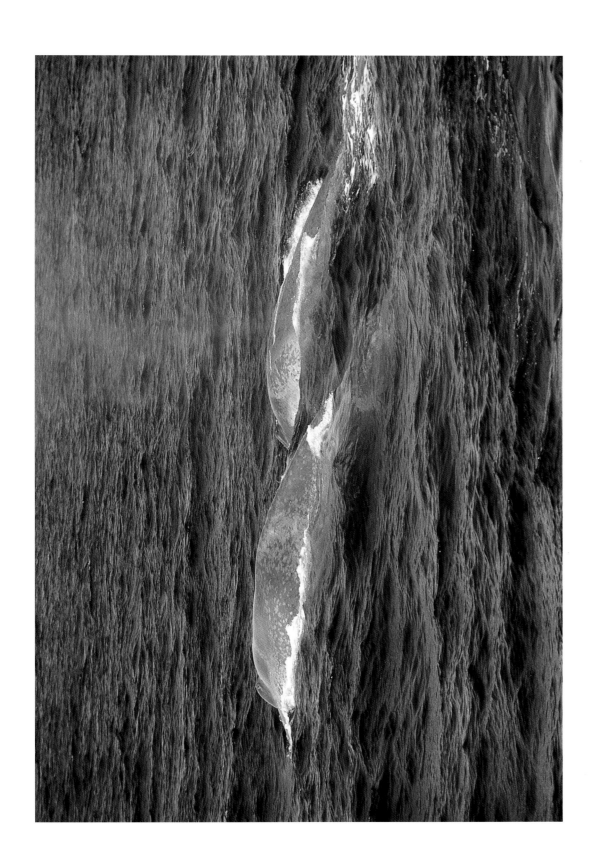

Although a hundred or more blue whales may feed within a region, they are usually alone or closely associated with one other animal.

The Survivors

There will again be whales of this size if mankind is successful in conserving the depleted and fragmented stocks. I shall not, however, be here to read about those greatest ones, for my generation has hunted down the whales and it will be my grandchildren's generation which (I hope) will see them return.

— Victor B. Scheffer, marine mammalogist

Although blue whale populations in most areas were decimated by commercial whaling, it is difficult to determine their population size, either at the end of whaling in 1965, or today. Counting whales is difficult because of their vast range and mobility, and because we can't see them when they are under water. The uncertainties that these difficulties create are the reasons (and the excuses) why whaling nations ignored the impact of their actions until it was too late.

Nowhere is this difficulty in estimating the size of the population more apparent than in the Antarctic. The waters of the southern hemisphere, particularly around Antarctica in the austral summer, were home to the largest blue whale population in the world. Prior to commercial whaling, it is likely that 200,000 blue whales fed in these waters. Yet it was not until the early 1960s that three independent scientists (aptly named the Committee of Three), who were appointed by the International Whaling Commission, published their findings. The results from analysis of all the whaling catch and effort data revealed that the surviving blue whale population in the Antarctic in 1963 numbered a mere 650 to 1950 animals. It was only with these stark findings that the IWC could finally agree to protect blue whales from hunting.

Several methods were used to estimate size of the surviving blue whale population. The primary method evaluated how quickly the effort to find and kill a blue whale (measured in 'catcher boat work days') increased as whales were killed. Essentially, this meant that if after killing 100,000 whales it required twice as much effort to catch a whale, then the population probably was 200,000 before the whaling. This approach was inaccurate because it did not account for a number of variables including changes in the methods and tools used to hunt whales and shifts in locations of whaling. It also relied on accurate whaling data, something that recent revelations of gross under reporting by the Soviet Union belie.

More than 30 years after their protection, the status and recovery of blue whale populations remain in question. Despite encouraging news from a few regions, they have shown little sign of recovery in most other areas.

However there has been a dramatic increase in blue whale numbers off the California coast. In our research, which began in the mid 1980s, we encountered concentrations of hundreds of blue whales there, far more than had been found in any surveys that had been conducted previously. On a single aerial survey in September 1996, we estimated more than 250 blue whales concentrated in a 50-mile (80-km) long area near the Farallon Islands, off San Francisco Bay, California. Blue whales were only rarely sighted from the Farallon Islands in the 1970s and only began to be seen more frequently in the 1980s. Changes in sightings of blue whales from survey ships along the California coast were examined by Jay Barlow, a scientist with

A blue whale dwarfs our research boat.

Blue whales and other baleen whales do not use echolocation to find their prey. Nevertheless, they are able to search the murky dark waters and locate dense swarms of krill.

45

The way whales sleep is very different to humans. Because they must think to breathe they are only able to rest one hemisphere of the brain at a time.

46

Southwest Fisheries Science Center in southern California. He found that the sighting rate was more than twice as high in 1991 compared to a decade earlier. These changes are too dramatic to be explained by population increase alone. Whale distribution must also have shifted to this area, perhaps because of a shift in the whales' prey.

Our research and that of Southwest Fisheries Science Center has recently revealed that about 2000 blue whales feed off California in the summer and fall. We think it is fairly accurate because it was made by two independent methods which produced similar numbers. We used mark-recapture methods based on photographs of identified whales and estimated that there were 2000 whales along the California and Mexico coast. This agreed with an alternate estimate made by Jay Barlow from large ship surveys using a technique called line-transect sampling. This method involved calculating the average density of blue whales off California by tallying the number seen along a set of systematic lines or transects. Both these estimates, that were only for a limited portion of the North Pacific, are surprisingly high – surprising because they are considerably larger than previous estimates for the entire North Pacific Ocean.

Nowhere has the lack of a recovery of blue whale populations been more apparent than on some of their former whaling grounds off Alaska. The waters off Akutan, Aleutian Islands, and Port Hobron, Kodiak Island, were prime whaling grounds for blue whales from 1917 to 1939. Because these were shore-based stations, the catcher boats caught most of the blue whales in a fairly small and well-defined area.

About 50 years after hunting of blue whales ceased from these two stations, several scientific expeditions conducted surveys to examine how blue whales had recovered in these regions. Not a single blue whale was seen during these surveys. Other whales were seen, but the species that was the focus of whaling in these waters is now either gone or extremely rare. Other

Alaskan waters, once the home of thousands of blue whales, are now only rarely visited by these great creatures.

What could explain the failure of this and other populations of blue whales to show a recovery? It is possible that blue whales were hunted to such low levels that a recovery, if it occurs, will take many years or even decades to be noticeable. There is also increasing evidence that blue whales may have been hunted for much longer than had been previously reported. Some of this may be the result of illegal hunting of blue whales by Soviet whalers; the full extent of the under reporting of blue whale catches has not been fully revealed.

To understand the status of blue whale populations it is necessary to consider how these populations are distributed and related to each other. Blue whales are found in all oceans of the world. Like most baleen whales, they make seasonal north-south migrations between cold water summer feeding areas and warm water wintering areas. Despite the whalers' intense interest in this species, blue whales were primarily hunted on their summer feeding grounds. Most of our knowledge about blue whale distribution and behavior comes from these areas. During the winter blue whales were more widely dispersed, less efficient to hunt, and yielded less oil when killed.

Blue whales from the northern and southern hemispheres visit their tropical wintering areas at opposite times of year, further separating the populations in the two hemispheres. For example, blue whales are feeding off California while their counterparts in the southern hemisphere are in tropical waters (where some mate and give birth to calves). When the northern hemisphere whales migrate southward along the coast of Mexico and beyond, the southern whales are swimming towards Antarctic waters to feed.

These long migrations of blue whales may not be universal, however. In the northern Indian Ocean, for example, there appears to be a year-round population of the smaller pygmy blue whale. A non-migratory population may

48

49

Photographs of the tail flukes sometimes show distinctive markings to aid identification of individual blue whales.

occur in one area of the eastern tropical Pacific, 600 miles (965 km) west of Central America, called the Costa Rican Dome, where whales have been seen in all seasons of the year. These sightings could reflect the presence of a resident population of blue whales, but it is more likely that this may be the wintering area for blue whales from both the northern and southern hemispheres, using the same area in different seasons.

The first direct information on blue whale migratory pathways and movements came from research during whaling. A Discovery tag, which was a uniquely numbered steel shaft, was shot into the blubber of whales during special expeditions. The tag was recovered only if the whale was later killed and the tag found during processing of the blubber. The locations where the whale was tagged and where it was killed could then be collated. There were problems with record keeping, however, and sometimes when a tag was found, it would be unclear from which animal it came.

Throats distended, two whales feed in unison.

In the Antarctic, over 900 of these tags were placed in blue whales and close to 100 were recovered. Many of these were found near the regions were they had been tagged, suggesting there were separate 'stocks' or subpopulations. There were a few examples of more dramatic movements, including one animal, killed two years after tagging, that had traveled to the opposite side of Antarctica. In the North Pacific, Discovery tags were also used, but only 16 recoveries were made. Because of this small sample, relatively little was learned about the movements and migrations of blue whales in the North Pacific. A few long-range movements were documented, however, including one from British Columbia to the Aleutian Islands.

Information on the long-range north-south migrations of blue whales in the southern hemisphere and the North Pacific has sometimes come from indirect methods. Blue whales on feeding grounds frequently carry or have scars from a variety of parasites, such as suckerfish, and certain barnacles that occur only in warm waters. The presence of these species and scars indicates that the whales spend at least part of the winter months in tropical waters.

Photographic identification of individuals has provided new information on the movements of blue whales. A pattern of movement has emerged along the coast of Mexico and California: some whales move from the Sea of Cortez in late winter and early spring to the west coast of Baja California, arriving in spring and early summer, then to the waters off California in summer and fall, and finally back to the west coast of Baja in late fall. Not all blue whales follow this pattern; even during the peak months of blue whale concentration off California, from July to November, there are still some animals off Baja California.

Blue whale movements along the coast of California are also variable. Resightings of the same whale often indicate that it has shifted location up and down the coast multiple times, and also moved from inshore to offshore. During this period they are searching for prey and feeding. The exact locations where they are found, and the time they spend in these areas, vary considerably. Sometimes they are widely distributed along the whole coast, while at other times they are concentrated in one area. These shifts can be dramatic; we can be conducting research in an area where there are hundreds of whales feeding, and then go out the following day to find that they have disappeared. They are fast swimmers and can move long distances quickly.

Although blue whales rarely breach, sometimes they leap halfway out of the water when they are traveling quickly.

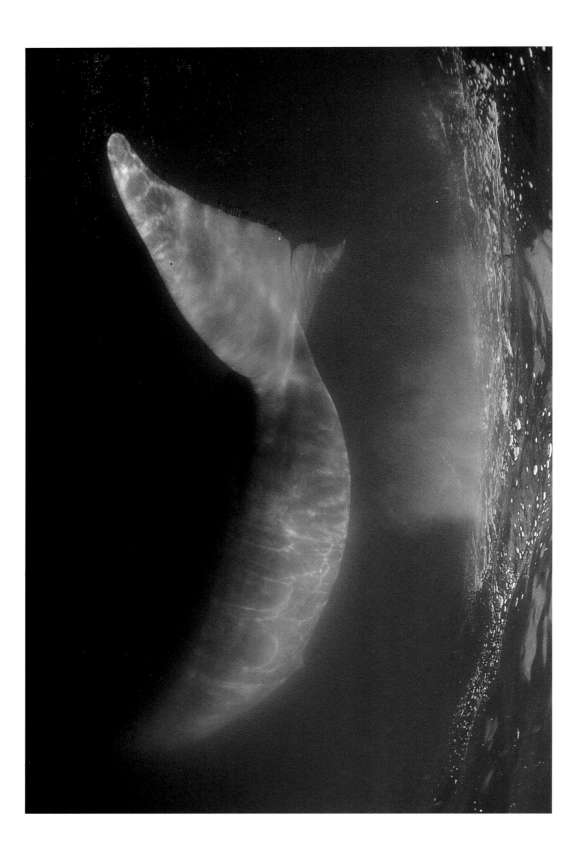

The Big Gulp

Blue whales migrate to colder, high-latitude areas in the summer and fall to feed on the rich swarms of prey that are seasonally abundant in these regions. Most of our information about what they eat comes from the examination of stomach contents of animals killed during whaling. More recently, we have collected blue whale feces from the water for identification of prey parts. Blue whales feed almost exclusively on krill, which are small, shrimp-like zooplankton. The giant species of this krill, *Euphausia superba*, is found in Antarctic waters and is only about 2.5 in (6.5 cm) long. The krill that blue whales eat off California are only about 1 in (2.5 cm) long. Blue whales also occasionally feed on other small organisms, such as pelagic red crabs. We have observed them off California feeding on fish, but this is very rare.

During these months of intense feeding, blue whales are storing energy in their blubber which can be used during the rest of the year. They feed very little during the migration and may fast in the winter while in tropical waters. In the Southern Hemisphere, most whales killed during this time had stomachs that were either empty or that contained very little krill. In the North Pacific, some feeding may occur in all seasons.

It is hard to believe that a creature as large as a blue whale could subsist almost exclusively on prey that is so small. It feeds by taking huge gulps of water which are filled with dense swarms of krill. The whale has 55-88 throat pleats which enable its throat to distend into a huge balloon from jaw to navel. It then pushes the water back out through fringed baleen plates with its enormous tongue. As the water is filtered out, the krill are captured in the baleen. A blue whale has between 270 and 400 of these parallel plates which are up to 3 ft (1 m) long and made of a fingernail-like keratin material.

There are no direct measurements of how much a blue whale can consume. However, if we make some rough calculations of the energy required by such a huge body, the numbers are staggering. Dale Rice, a biologist with the National Marine Mammal Laboratory, estimates that a 75-80-ton whale needs about 1.5 million calories a day. Because blue whales may feed intensely for only half the year, the daily consumption on the feeding grounds is probably more like 3 million calories, or 4 tons of krill per day. The type of krill found off California weighs about one tenth of a gram, so that would mean that the daily consumption of one blue whale would be 40 million krill. A blue whale stomach has been estimated to hold 1-2 tons of krill at one time.

Blue whales feed at different depths, depending on the location of the krill. Most of them are concentrated from the surface to a depth of several hundred feet. When blue whales feed at these deeper depths, they dive repeatedly in the same area, staying submerged for up to 15 minutes (though whalers reported much longer dives). When they are feeding at the surface, we are often captivated by spectacular surface lunge feeding, including the following observation which we made in 1988.

We had read accounts from the whaling days of blue whales seen off Magdalena Bay along the west coast of Baja California. Taking a small inflatable boat loaded with fuel cans, a tent and some food, we set up camp along the coast and headed off on a quest to find them. We searched for days and days, to the north, south, and to banks well offshore. We saw a couple of humpbacks and some false killer whales, but no blue whales. Low on fuel, we thought our hunt was over, when not only did we find blue whales, but we found ourselves caught in the middle of about 40 of them feeding on pelagic red crabs. These small red crustaceans are about 3 in (8 cm) long, look like lobsters and appear in immense swarms. We were leaning over the side of the boat looking through the clear water at what seemed to be millions of them as deep as we could see. Suddenly, they all opened up their pinchers in a threatened pose. The huge open jaws of a blue whale rose from the depths and engulfed the tiny creatures, which had little hope of doing much damage

When blue whales feed at the surface they often roll over on their sides and swim along with their mouths open.

57

with such tiny weapons to such a large predator as this. Although the boat's engine was running, which usually alerts whales to our presence, we realized that we were surrounded by gigantic whales with very large mouths; they seemed totally oblivious to us. Open mouths with bulging throat pleats filled with thousands of gallons of water were breaking the surface on all sides of us. A 13-ft (4 m) inflatable boat and its two occupants would fit in one of these mouths easily. But to be amidst this incredible feeding process was fascinating; it was really hard to leave. Finally, our fuel situation forced the issue, and we went back to the closest town and got lots more. We spent four more glorious days with this group, and were able to obtain good identification shots and witness more of this amazing feeding behavior.

When blue whales are feeding at the surface, birds, fish and other marine mammals often congregate in the same area to take advantage of the feast. Thousands of marine birds of a variety of species including Cassin's auklets, phalaropes, and shearwaters, all of which also feed on krill, flock to the area. These birds often take advantage of the krill that whales help to bring to the surface. Several species of dolphins and porpoises, including Pacific white-sided dolphins and Dall's porpoise, often 'bow ride' in front of blue whales, possibly using this as a feeding strategy.

Female blue whales need to feed heavily so that they can store reserves for reproduction. Details of the reproduction of this species are something of a mystery. We know that breeding occurs during winter in tropical waters, but we are not really sure where. It is possible that whales are widely distributed so that large concentrations do not occur in one area. Whales must be far from land because nearshore sightings of them during this time are rare. We do not know how mates find each other, how mates are selected, or whether there is much competition. Most of what we do know about reproduction comes from the dead animals that were examined during whaling.

Although the time that a blue whale mother cares for her calf is short, the physical demands are gigantic. In the Antarctic population, a female becomes sexually mature when she is about five years old and 79 ft (24 m) long. Conception takes

Throat pleats allow the blue whale's throat to expand and engulf huge quantities of krill.

59

A mother and her calf remain close together for seven months.

A researcher circles a surfacing whale.

place in the winter, and it takes about a year for the fetus to develop. The following winter she gives birth to one calf that is 23 ft (7 m) long and weighs 3 tons. She nurses it with milk that is 35-50% fat and the consistency of loose, runny cheese. During this time, she relies heavily on the fat that was stored during the previous summer and fall. She and her calf swim thousands of miles to the colder, plankton-rich waters. There, the calf shifts from its mother's milk to krill when it is about seven months old. It has grown to a length of 53 ft (16 m) and has gained about 20 tons (it now weighs 23 tons). Each day while it was nursing, the calf has grown almost 1.5 in (4 cm) and gained 200 lb (90 kg). The mother has lost about 50 tons, or about one-third of her body weight. The long ridge of her backbone protrudes above the rest of her body, as she is visibly thin. Now it is time for her to rebuild her fat reserves. It is also the time when mothers and their calves separate. This female may breed in the following winter and begin the process all over again.

Except for the seven-month bond between mothers and their calves, blue whales tend to have a solitary existence. They rarely spend time in large groups and are usually either alone or in a pair. These pairings probably allow blue whales to be more efficient in swimming and in catching prey. Surprisingly, preliminary findings indicate these pairs are usually a male and a female. This suggests that, even on the feeding grounds, these pairings may have a role in courtship. On the rare occasions when three blue whales are close together; they often engage in a 'racing' behavior; they swim at speeds of about 15 knots, often leaping out of the water with their heads and creating huge waves and spray. They roll on their sides and swim very close together. This behavior can continue for hours, but eventually results in one of the three breaking off from the group.

Despite their size, blue whales have to be vigilant of killer whales. Several attacks have been witnessed. Killer whales swim fast enough to keep up with blue whales and work as a pack to subdue and kill large prey. They often do not wait to kill a blue whale to begin feeding, but tear away strips of blubber and pieces of the tongue or lips. The blue whale continues to try to dive and escape from the attacking whales. When attacking certain other species, we think killer whales probably focus their attacks on young or sick animals. This may also be the case for blue whales; we have seen many of them with scars in the shape of killer whale teeth. Based on the number of whales we see with these scars, it appears that many of these attacks are not fatal.

A number of creatures make their existence off blue whales and usually live on only one or a few species of whales. Several species of barnacles attach themselves to appendages including the flukes and dorsal fin. Small diatoms

This whale has a badly damaged tail fluke.

A lungeing blue whale creates a huge splash after surfacing.

form a thin slimy layer on the skin of blue whales, especially along their undersides. Specialized species of sucker-fish or remoras attach themselves to the sides of blue whales and feed on sloughed skin and remains of the whales' prey as they catch a free ride.

The life span of blue and other baleen whales is poorly known. With many toothed animals, including toothed whales, annual layers on teeth provide one of the best aging techniques. With baleen whales, this is not possible. The best method has been to examine the wax-like plug in their ears, which can be removed from a dead whale; since a set number of layers are added each year, the age of the whale can be determined by counting these zones. Unfortunately there appears to be some irregularity in the formation of these layers, especially in younger animals, and the layers are harder to count in older whales.

Life spans of 70 years or more have been documented in several species, while evidence for an even longer maximum life span for some whales has recently been discovered. A harpoon head that had not been in common usage for over 100 years was recently found in a bowhead whale, suggesting this animal had been alive at least that long. In the future, long-term photo-identification research will provide a better understanding of the mortality rate and, eventually, the life span of blue whales.

Because it is so hard to determine the age of a whale, some huge miscalculations were made during whaling related to the age of first reproduction. At one time it was thought that blue whales were sexually mature when they were only two years old. (blue whales become sexually mature at five years or older) and that the reproductive rate of blue and other large whales would increase in response to whaling, something that did not occur.

Both of these overly optimistic assumptions created a false belief that whales could recover from the decimation of whaling much more rapidly than was actually the case.

The blow of a whale, which reaches 30 ft (9 m) into the air, is expelled from lungs that weigh over a ton.

65

The Future

It is an exciting time to be studying blue whales. Until the mid 1960s, most of what we knew about them came as a grisly byproduct of commercial whaling. Once blue whales were protected, little research was conducted for many years: there was no financial incentive to learn more and no whaling ships from which data could be collected. Blue whales were also considered so rare that it would require a huge effort just to find them, let alone gather enough data to be scientifically meaningful. In the 1980s that situation began to change, and recently a number of new research projects have been undertaken.

The development of photographic identification of individual whales has revolutionized the study of many species of large cetaceans and will likely be an important basis for future research. One of the exciting aspects of photographic identification is that the value of the method increases over time as detailed sighting histories of individual animals are compiled. Though this technique has been useful in the study of movements of whales and population size, this is only the beginning. With long-term data we can now examine population trends, individual reproductive histories, associations among animals and survival rates.

Genetic studies are just starting to explore how populations of blue whales are related and structured. Samples of an animal's skin are collected to examine the patterns of DNA. Most samples are taken using a small biopsy dart that is shot from a cross-bow. Basic information such as gender can be determined from this research, which can help us to understand more about the social structure and behavior of the whales, and also answer many questions about how whales from different regions are related. It can help solve past controversies about the status of the three subspecies, including the pygmy blue whale, without the political pressures imposed in the past by whaling interests.

Other new research is investigating the underwater life of blue whales and may provide clues about how they find their prey. Radio tags equipped with a pressure sensor, attached to the back of a blue whale, provide information on the movements of the whale and the depth to which it is diving. Multiple-frequency sonar provides a sophisticated picture of the distribution of prey under water and gives information on how whales move and feed in relation to the distribution of krill.

Long range movements of blue whales are also being examined with satellite radio tags attached to animals. Those undertaking these studies face the enormous challenge of how to attach the tags to such fast-swimming animals. The tags can transmit information about the location and dive times of the whale, and provide precise details on the tagged whale's travel, including perhaps the presently unknown information on where whales go to breed.

The acoustic world of the blue whale is the subject of intensive new research. Military hydrophone arrays, formerly used solely for tracking submarines, have now been made available for scientific research on whales. To interpret this information, many questions need to be answered about the vocal behavior of blue whales. Why do they vocalize, is it to navigate, communicate, or locate prey? Once we understand more about these vocalizations, monitoring these sounds from afar could reveal a lot about this species.

Although survival of the blue whale as a species may not be as in doubt as it was 30 years ago, many challenges still lie ahead. Because they are hard to study, have a long life span and low reproductive rate, whales will always be poor candidates for exploitation regardless of how our attitudes change. Management will be difficult because they roam the oceans without regard for international borders. People may be tempted to exploit whales and reap short-term benefits even though hunting may not be sustainable.

Unfortunately, current threats to whales and other marine creatures are less visible and harder to document than whaling. Many of these threats,

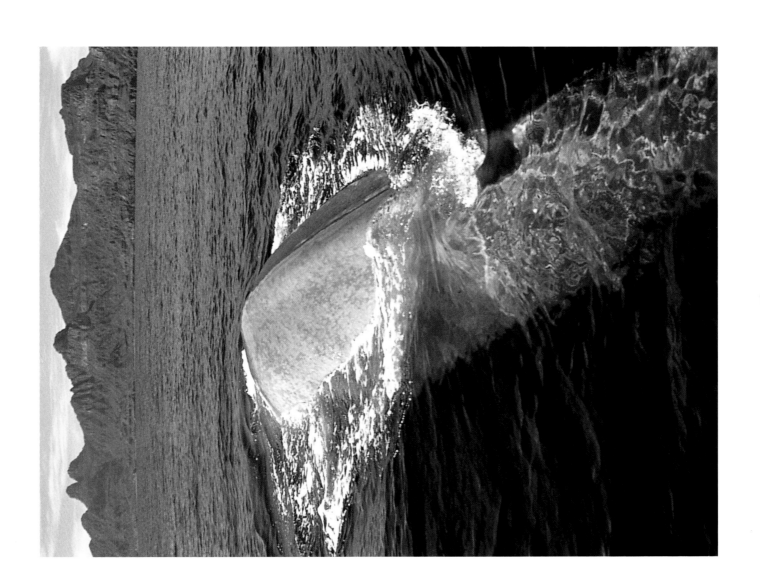

however, are no less deadly. Entanglement in fishing gear has become a major source of mortality of many marine mammals. A number of species, including the vaquita and several river dolphins, hover on the brink of extinction largely as a consequence of accidental mortality related to fishing. Fortunately, relatively blue whales have been killed due to entanglements in nets.

Blue whales and other marine mammals rely on the sea for their food. Long-lived contaminants that are sprayed on crops, or industrial chemicals that are discarded, often eventually end up in the sea. The oceans have also been used as dumping grounds for pollutants. Marine mammals, especially coastal seals and dolphins, are exposed to high concentrations of contaminants. Some species are so contaminated that their tissues could qualify as toxic waste. This problem is most severe for species like killer whales that feed high in the food chain and are exposed to the highest levels of contaminants. Even lower levels of contaminants, however, can have subtle impacts, such as causing immuno-suppression which makes animals more susceptible to disease.

History has demonstrated an incredible change in the attitude people have towards whales. At the beginning of the twentieth century, people viewed the world as one of unlimited resources; the seas were full of life. But the hundreds of thousands of whales that once roamed the world's oceans were decimated in a flurry that was swift and unrelenting. In the last 30 years, however, most of the world has shifted from a view of whales as a commodity to one where they are revered and protected.

Although our world has been spared from the loss of the largest species ever to have lived on it, other species and entire habitats are disappearing every day. 'Save the whales' may be a more popular slogan than 'save the krill' or 'save the ocean', but they are all inexorably linked. To many, whales inspire a sense of awe and excitement, but to protect them we must take a broader view. The only way we can ensure their survival is to think of them as symbols for the entire ecosystem, something on which both whales and ultimately ourselves are dependent.

Once thought to be the last of a vanishing breed, the blue whale's future now appears to be brighter.

Blue Whale Facts

Scientific name:
Balaenoptera musculus

Heaviest:	over 200 tons
Width of tail-fluke:	25 ft (8 m)
Swimming speed:	avg: 10-12 knots, fastest: 20 knots
Longevity:	70 years or more
Age at sexual maturity:	5-10 years
Gestation:	11-12 months
Calving interval:	usually once every 2-3 years
Size of newborn calf:	25 ft (7m) long, 3 tons
Size of weaned calf:	53 ft (16 m) long, 23 tons
Calf age at weaning:	7 months
Distribution:	Blue whales occur in all oceans of the world. They feed in high latitude regions during the summer and fall; they migrate to tropical waters in the winter where some whales breed or give birth to calves.

Biographical Note

John Calambokidis is a Senior Research Biologist and co-founder (in 1979) of Cascadia Research, a non-profit organization. Besides blue whales, his research has evaluated contaminant impacts on marine mammals and examined the biology of humpback and gray whales. He loves the challenge of conducting research far offshore in a small boat.

Gretchen Steiger has been a Research Biologist with Cascadia Research since 1983. She has conducted research on marine mammals in many regions from the Arctic to Costa Rica. She and her husband, John Calambokidis, first met while studying marine mammals in Alaska. They live in Olympia, Washington, with their 5-year-old-son.

Recommended Reading

The Blue Whale by George L. Small, Columbia University Press, New York, 1971. Winner of the National Book Award in 1972, this book was the first to popularize the plight of blue whales and document the tragic history of modern whaling.

The Stocks of Whales by N. A. Mackintosh, Fishing News (Books) Ltd., London, 1965 A comprehensive review of the biological discoveries made during whaling in the Antarctic.

The Natural History of Whales and Dolphins by Peter G. Evans, Facts of File Publications, New York, 1987. A detailed review of the biology of cetaceans.